Don't Solo Travel Until You Read This

Every Solo Traveler Hand Book

Penny J. Cooper

Table Of Contents

INTRODUCTION

Embark on a journey of self-discovery and exploration with our comprehensive Solo Travel Guide – your ultimate companion to embracing the world as a fearless and independent adventurer. In these pages, you'll uncover the art of navigating new landscapes solo, forging connections with diverse cultures, and immersing yourself in unforgettable experiences. Whether you're a seasoned globetrotter or a first-time solo traveler, this guide is your passport to unlocking the transformative power of venturing alone. Prepare to ignite your wanderlust, conquer your uncertainties, and craft your very own narrative of discovery on the road less traveled.

Traveling alone can help you build your confidence, learn more about the world, try things you wouldn't do with a buddy or partner, and meet people from all walks of life. Traveling alone is getting more and more common, and some places are ideal for it! We've included all of our best solo travel ideas and recommendations in one place for you.

Utilize our tips in this solo travel guide to organize your trip and increase your comfort level when seeing new places by yourself. We think you'll like the independence!

Chapter 1: Reasons You Should Try Solo Travel Now

Still not convinced that traveling alone is right for you? As long as you set your mind to it and push yourself to attempt new things, you can accomplish it and have a blast. Here are 27 reasons why you should embark on solo traveling now, with no further delay;

Complete freedom:

Although having friends around is helpful, traveling in groups often necessitates sacrificing your plans. Traveling alone is luxurious. It's all about you and accomplishing your objectives.

Meet incredible individuals:

It's simple to make friends if you know how. Stepping outside of your comfort zone and gaining the courage to approach strangers are key components of solo travel.

Study various cultures:

The purpose of travel is to widen your horizons and become more compassionate. You'll be connecting with people from all walks of life as a solo traveler. Who knows what fascinating facts about their ethnicity, religion, or culture you'll learn?

Gain experience in life:

The most difficult challenges in life may be conquered with the precious assistance of life experience. Even better, it helps you seem intriguing and employable on your resume.

Respect yourself:

Do you feel at ease with yourself? Can you feel at ease in your environment? To "find themselves" and investigate their identities, many individuals go on solitary trips. You'll also come to understand that you don't need someone else to make you feel whole while you're living alone.

Boost your mental well-being

Being alone is therapeutic for the spirit and may even help you cope with issues like stress, worry, and sadness. A little alone time might be beneficial for health for people who work in high-stress workplaces or anybody who wants a change of scenery.

Acquire social abilities:

As a lone traveler, you'll rapidly learn how to strike up discussions and keep connections. Your communication skills will improve as a result, which is great for maintaining ties with family members back home.

Have empathy and compassion:

The secret to being more empathic is to open your mind and heart to other people and to comprehend their way of life and their struggles. Travel may help bridge the gap between cultures, which can be mostly caused by ignorance and inexperience.

Become more adept at solving issues:

Diverse skill sets makeup diverse groups. But you'll have to work things out for yourself. If you can't mend the hole in your jacket or figure out bus schedules in a foreign language, no one will ask. You'll be very good at problem-solving when you go back, and you may use those abilities at work.

Make choices in life:

Those who are forceful and natural leaders rise to the top and take charge in groups. Therefore, less active people are less likely to get their talents recognized. You'll be responsible for making all the choices on your own, so developing this ability is crucial.

Accept your shortcomings:

No one is flawless, but recognizing our shortcomings is an excellent place to start when trying to better oneself. Traveling alone gives you the chance to discover more about yourself and identify any areas for development.

Discover new languages:

When you travel alone, you have the ideal chance to expand your linguistic repertoire. You'll need to figure out how to speak with others when you're outside of your comfort zone, and the best way to do so is to learn a few useful words and sentences for discussion.

Become one with nature:

An opportunity to connect with nature may be had while traveling alone. Numerous conservation volunteer initiatives might allow you to see the world while giving back to the environment if you wish to learn more about the environment.

Be completely independent:

Your ability to live, work, or volunteer alone in a foreign location can help you become more independent. This is excellent life training for individuals who are used to depending on their parents or other family members for financial help.

Discover a higher purpose in life:

When you see wild creatures in their natural environment or learn about the lives of people in underdeveloped areas, your appreciation for life will surge. This may give you a profound sense of connection to the rest of the planet and the people or creatures that inhabit it.

Turn off the technology:

Through our electronics, we are constantly linked to the world we live in. Embrace the absence of 4G or WiFi while visiting isolated regions so that you may be fully present and at one with your surroundings.

Support regional communities:

Tourism boosts local economies, and even little expenses like taxi fares or a snack from a street vendor help people provide for their families. Through initiatives like coaching youth sports teams or teaching English to children, you may also have an impact on the lives of those you come into contact with.

Eat cuisine from many countries:

One of the things that binds us together is food, so learning about the specialties and cuisines of various nations can be an intriguing adventure.

Improve your ability to say "yes":

Once you've gone solo, you'll become used to saying "yes" to more opportunities. Your life may become more open as a result of new interests, sports, activities, and cultural journeys that lead you to far-off locales.

Get out of the way:

You simply cannot immerse yourself in the local culture or go down lesser-traveled routes during holidays. Traveling alone will force you to take risks and expose you to experiences not found in travel guides. A host family will be able to show you the world in the most genuine manner possible if you stay with them.

Discover global history:

Get the opportunity to discover more about other nations, their history, their customs, and historical tales. An excellent approach to visiting all the key sights is via organized trips.

Spend money wisely:

Once you've lived the backpacker lifestyle, you'll have better financial sense. This is the ideal moment to learn how to handle your own money if you have never done so.

Boost your physical fitness:

Spend more time organizing athletic activities rather than gatherings centered on drinking or eating out. Make sure you keep active every day while still leaving time to unwind with folks you meet along the route. A trekking vacation might be a great way to get your fitness routine off to a good start.

Become more intuitive:

Solo travelers must be vigilant and observant at all times, and you'll learn along the route to trust your instincts about whom to believe.

Make enduring friendships:

Not everyone has the good fortune to meet their closest friends in their hometown or at their place of education. However, many people can have profound and significant interactions with other travelers. You can count on a buddy for life if you have similar interests and morals.

Learning blogging

While traveling alone enables us to unplug from technology, it also allows us to utilize it for productive purposes like writing and storytelling. You won't ever have to worry about being lonely on your trip if you tell people about your adventures. Through online networks, this may also be a terrific way to make new travel friends.

Boost your imagination:

Traveling can inspire you so much, whether you're a creative industry professional or a student of the arts. You'll have more time to savor the sights and get a full sense of each location without a constant companion at your side.

Chapter 2: Solo Travel Tips You Must Know

- ## Tips For Solo Travel Before You Leave;

1.Booking high-quality travel insurance with excess protection that is valid in the nation you're traveling to is the most crucial thing to do before you travel. In case you misplace your phone or other gadgets, we also advise buying protection for them.

2. Use the Duolingo app to prepare by learning the fundamentals of the local tongue. You can learn some useful phrases that are simple to remember from it, and you never know when you might need them.

3. Put money aside and budget enough money for your trip. To enjoy your trip, you don't want to run out of supplies while traveling.

4. Travel light and pack smart. Without a large suitcase, getting about is much simpler! Don't forget the necessities, including medicine, sunblock, and bug spray. Check out our comprehensive packing list for ideas.

- **Selection A Destination**

5. Take into account nations that are friendly to solitary travelers when choosing where to go on your vacation alone. The top criteria to consider are safety, cost, accessibility, whether English is a common language, and communities of other travelers. Here are some of our best suggestions for solo travel.

6. Do a ton of research on the area you're going to so you know how to get around, what to do when you get to the airport, and what the best attractions are.

7. It's best to establish a basic plan and make as many reservations as you can in advance if you're going on a short vacation of up to three weeks. You'll want to see and do as much as you can because time is limited. For longer journeys, feel free to book items as you go for more flexibility.

8. Bear in mind that your expenses will be higher than if you were traveling with a companion. Hotels, rental cars, and some excursions are examples of things you'll need to pay in full for.

9. Taking your first vacation alone? Why not consider taking a quick city holiday to Berlin, Barcelona, Lisbon, or Vienna? Before making a significant vacation arrangement, you can experience solo travel in all of these fantastic cities.

10. When planning your first solo trip, don't be scared to choose a place you've been before and are familiar with. By yourself, it might be an entirely different experience.

- **Places To Stay As A Solo Traveler;**

11. You can meet lots of other travelers at hostels, many of whom are solo travelers. Before making a reservation, always read the reviews for the hostel. Location, price, and the hostel's social activities and age range are all crucial factors.

12. In addition to communal rooms, many hostels also provide individual rooms. Private hostel rooms are ideal if you want your own space but also enjoy the communal atmosphere of a hostel. They are more expensive than a dorm but still less expensive than hotels.

13. Resist the urge to book a hostel room. Go for it if you want a couple of nights in a five-star hotel or a private AirBnB property with a kitchen! With a full night's sleep and some time away from the hostel environment, you may relax in the swimming pool and indulge in as much spa time as you'd like.

14. Whenever possible, lock away your stuff in the hotel safe or private lockers at the hostel. Reduce any holiday hassles by keeping your belongings secure, especially your passport and cash.

15. Do you know what couch surfing is? You can stay with a local for free or at a very low cost at their home or apartment. It's a cool travel idea. It's highly regarded among lone travelers and a fantastic opportunity to connect with informed locals! Just make sure to pick a host that has a lot of past visitors and positive reviews.

16. Confirm that the lodging you are reserving offers free WiFi. It's necessary for studying your location and keeping in touch with friends and family back home.

Eating Out;

17. It can be difficult to eat your first dinner by yourself in a restaurant. Don't listen to the voices in your head that accuse you of being odd for dining alone. It is a typical aspect of traveling! Travelers on business, lone travelers, and you may all do it with ease. If you're truly anxious about dining alone, try to pick a place that's unassuming and quiet the first time.

18. Meeting other travelers in the common areas and making plans for a night out are important aspects of the hostel culture. Simply inquire as to what others are doing for dinner, and you may be able to join a small group or find a fellow traveler at your hostel who will be happy to accompany you to the restaurant.

19. A lot of hostels provide 'family' dinners' when everyone gathers and pays a one-time cost for drinks and delectable local food. Look for local hostels that provide this amenity; from our experience, it's great!

20. Prepare your meals in the kitchen of your hostel or apartment. You can use inventive cooking techniques and inexpensive local ingredients.

21. For quick, inexpensive meals on the go, take advantage of fast food establishments and street stalls. Additionally, it doesn't have to be harmful! If you look around, you can generally get fast food from a range of cuisines. The 'Cheap Eats' section of TripAdvisor is a good resource.

22. Go to a restaurant more than once if you genuinely enjoy it and feel comfortable dining alone. You can converse with the staff and sample new items from the menu.

23. To avoid crowds, eat early in the evening.

24. If the bar staff isn't too busy, eat by the bar and start a conversation with them.

25. Enroll in a group cooking class to learn how to prepare regional dishes with others. At a shared table, you will all eat together and develop your cooking abilities.

- **Exploring Your Destination;**

26. Go on organized tours to see the sights in the area with other like-minded tourists. Tours are a fantastic opportunity to make new friends and learn interesting facts about a place from a local. You may find them in practically any tourist

location in the world, whether they are long multi-day guided tours or a brief day or half-day excursions. For multi-day tour schedules, look into Tour Radar or Viator, respectively.

27. Before making a tour reservation, always read tour reviews. We advise using TripAdvisor. To get the greatest deal and observe what kind of crowd the tour draws, you might also want to

compare shops. Younger "budget travelers" will be on some trips, while history buffs and perhaps couples will be on others. Pick what fits you best!

28. While tours are fantastic for networking and sharing your experience, we also advise independent exploration. You'll genuinely get to appreciate your environment without any

interruptions, and it's calming and enlightening. Visit a remote temple on your own, or get up early to catch the sunrise while sightseeing in the city.

29. Explore your destination's less-traveled regions by going off the beaten path. While the

most popular tourist attractions are wonderful, occasionally a less crowded location can provide a more exhilarating experience. There are hidden treasures everywhere!

30. Are you going to the Sagrada Familia in Barcelona or the Roman Colosseum? Purchase tickets online in advance to skip the line. You

won't have to spend as much time waiting in lines by yourself. The same is true for making travel arrangements and popular eateries.

31. Rise early and take your time exploring your destination. You can do anything you want, whenever you want, as you are alone and don't have to care about anyone else's schedule. Visit

the key sights early in the day when they are less crowded.

- **Traveling Around;**

32. Become familiar with the local transportation network. Compared to taking a cab, traveling alone is much cheaper and occasionally faster.

33. To reduce waiting times for luggage or the possibility of forgetting a suitcase, try to travel light with just one bag.

34. When traveling night buses or coaches, be cautious of your personal space and goods. Try to find a seat at the front of the bus where it's open.

35. Spend the extra money on an Uber or cab if you're genuinely unclear about where you're heading or if it's late at night. You'll arrive home promptly and safely.

36. Where possible, choose Uber (or a comparable taxi app) over the local taxi service. Given that trips are logged and drivers are registered, it is frequently safer than a regular cab. They are also less likely to defraud you!

37. Always arrive at the airport, railway station, or bus station with plenty of time to spare before departure, and allow enough time between modes of transportation. Being stuck alone is the last thing you want to happen!

38. Save an offline map of the location you're visiting to your Google Maps app. It functions without WiFi or your data signal and will guide you if you get lost. Additionally, we advise marking significant landmarks on the map, such as bars and restaurants. Visit our pals at The Travel Hack for guidance on how to achieve this.

39. Take a fully charged USB power pack with you when you go on trips or go camping. When the battery runs out, it will recharge your phone and is excellent for emergencies. The Anker PowerCore Redux power bank is what we use. Check out solar chargers as another useful device.

40. Bring a little daypack with you when you go out. Sunscreen, a little towel, a drink, and snacks are always useful!

41. Attempting to score a free upgrade on a flight when alone is the ideal scenario! At the check-in counter, enquire if the flight is busy and politely inquire about upgrading options. The airline will find it much simpler to obtain a nicer seat if you're traveling alone.

- **Safety Advice For Solo Travelers;**

42. When you're alone, exercise additional caution. If you're traveling with a friend or partner, you'll always have someone to aid you if you fall sick, but if you're traveling alone, you might not. Always keep a list of the closest hospitals handy, and be cautious about what you consume and any potentially risky situations. If you're going into the bush, try to travel with someone else.

43. Always keep a small first aid kit with you, complete with bandages, basic medications, and anti-dehydration sachets. This one from Amazon is what we use. One of our advice for solo travelers is that it works in every circumstance, even if you aren't going it alone.

44. When it gets dark out, don't go out alone, and when it does, stay in well-lit locations.

45. Know your limitations and don't overindulge whether drinking or out on the town. When arranging a night out, try to establish friends with other travelers who can keep an eye out for you.

46. Exercise caution when using cash and credit cards. You won't have a friend to ask for a loan of money if you run out of money or misplace your card. Always have a little extra cash in your bag or hidden in your hotel or hostel room.

47. Always keep a few friends or family members back home informed of your whereabouts. Changing your destination or preparing for a nighttime hike? In the unlikely event that something occurs, quickly notify them by sending them a message. It's also a good idea to let them know your itinerary before you go.

48. Write down your emergency contact information and carry it with you at all times in your wallet or purse.

49. Be aware of unexpected strangers who approach you on the street and try to sell you something. Even though they may appear kind, keep your guard up, and don't be hesitant to politely decline their advances.

50. Avoid flashing expensive phones and cameras in shady places, and crowded streets, especially at night. Also, avoid using headphones that block off background noise.

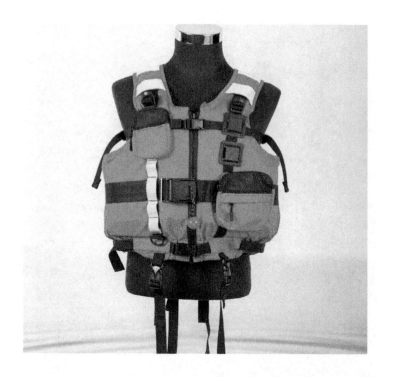

51. Always wear life jackets and helmets when available, and reserve excursions with recognized businesses with a strong safety record. We advise reading up on the business online before making a reservation.

52. When meeting someone for the first time, avoid disclosing too much personal information about yourself. Your whole name, the address where you're staying, and any priceless items you're carrying could be included.

53. Purchase a flat-pack money belt like the one we already use. It's perfect for securely storing your phone, cash, and ID and will fit neatly around your waist and under your shirt.

- **Advantages Of Meeting New People When Traveling Alone;**

54. The ideal place to meet other travelers is in a hostel, where social interaction is encouraged. There are a ton of other solo travelers who share your interests. Convert together with your roommates, in the common area, or during a scheduled hostel event. While some hostels promote a communal atmosphere, others are

quieter and more hotel-like. To get a sense of the spirit of the hostel, read the reviews in advance.

55. You have a fantastic opportunity to get to know the locals when you travel alone. Ask a local tour guide for advice, strike up a conversation at the bar, or strike up a conversation with bystanders at the market or a tourist attraction. Usually, a person's initial response will give you a good indication of whether or not they desire to be approached. A little bit of the local tongue may go a long way, and people will respect you for taking the time to learn it.

56. Regularly frequenting a café or dropping by one to catch up on emails and social media is a terrific method to meet people in a laid-back setting. Locate a coffee shop where there are lots of travelers.

57. Our preferred method of meeting new people is through organized tours. The entire day will be spent with them, and there will be numerous possibilities for dialogue.

58. Participate in a planned bar crawl with your hostel or the nightlife promoter in your community. Everyone becomes more laid back when they drink, and you can form bonds over a few beers in a bar. Simply don't drink too much!

59. You may get advice or set up a meetup in many locations' online travel forums and expat organizations. Look up your destination on Facebook, Reddit, and the Lonely Planet forums.

60. It's simple to meet people while traveling alone. Starting a discussion is the hardest part! You can start a conversation with anyone by using any of the following terrific methods, and you'll quickly find that it comes naturally to you. Top topics for conversation:

Request advice about the area you're in and find out when people arrived.

Ask inquiries and discuss their native nation or yours.

Ask someone who speaks the same language or with a familiar accent where they are from.

Find out if they are aware of any hip restaurants or cafes in the area. Even asking to join you is possible!

Inquire about their travel experience and whether they have any particular favorite locations.

Encourage them to talk about something cool they're doing or wearing. such as their necklace? Inquire about the retailer they used.

Be amiable and smile! It's the finest advice to follow in any social setting, and it will make you seem more personable.

61. You'll likely run across some nasty or annoying people, and not everyone you encounter will want to engage in a conversation. Don't take it personally and just move on to a more approachable and open individual.

- **General Advice For Solo Travelers To Ensure An Awesome Trip!;**

62. Don't be frightened to be alone, in contrast to our prior list of advice for traveling alone. You can develop your character on your vacation by being by yourself, and you can find tranquility in your own company. On your journey, spend as much or as little time alone as you like. After all, you are traveling alone.

63. Have you ever seen the film "Yes Man"? Prepare for your solo vacation by being impulsive and saying "yes" to (nearly) everything!

64. On a similar topic, feel free to decline invitations to join a group dinner or activity if you prefer to go your own way. It will be simple for you to make friends with other travelers but don't forget to focus on what brought you there in the first place.

65. When you're alone, it's simple to use your phone a lot to contact people back home. Try to limit your Facebook and Instagram usage. You

will be able to embrace the solitary travel lifestyle, have fun on your journey, and meet new people if you can temporarily cut yourself off from the outer world. Save using your phone until evenings when you're relaxed in your room.

66. Capture every moment of your journey with photos, including keeping a daily travel journal. You'll be better able to recall your journey in the future as well as the people you met. Asking passersby to snap your photo is nothing to be terrified of.

67. Exercise caution, but not excessive caution. Although it's necessary to be alert of your surroundings and the people you run into, most travels are trouble-free, so your main priority should be to have fun at all times!

68. Take a break; don't overwork yourself. Obtain some rest.

There are several benefits to traveling alone, including the freedom from coordinating schedules and the opportunity to focus only on your interests. Additionally, many locations have simple transit, a wide variety of activities, and generally secure environs, making them perfect for solo exploration. Here are a few of the world's most accommodating places for travelers traveling alone.

Beaver Creek, Colorado

This picturesque mountain community in the Rocky Mountains has something to offer all year long for people who like being outside. At Denver International Airport, board an Epic Mountain Express shuttle and drive 130 miles west to your hotel, house, or apartment. You won't have any problem traveling on your own since Beaver Creek property provides a complimentary shuttle service for travel around the property.

In the summer months, take advantage of lonely hiking, mountain biking, and relaxing by a tranquil mountain stream. In the winter, ski, and snowboard to your heart's delight. Don't miss out on neighborhood eateries like Citrea, which is influenced by the Mediterranean, Beaver Creek Chophouse, and Beano's Cabin (which you can visit on horseback).

Grand Cayman, Cayman Islands

Grand Cayman is accessible and reasonably priced by several U.S. airlines. It is known for its hospitable natives and excellent food, the latter of which has caused many to refer to the Cayman Islands as the gastronomic capital of the Caribbean. This island has lots of activities for those seeking solitude and it's easy to travel using taxis, rental cars, or public transportation.

A charter to Stingray City is a must if you want to interact with stingrays while they hunt for food. Another must-do is to go scuba diving or snorkeling with one of the more than 40 tour companies, such as Ocean Frontiers. To spend as much time in the water as possible, stay at the all-inclusive scuba diving resort Pirates Point Resort, or relax at opulent hotels like the Kimpton Seafire Resort + Spa on Seven Mile Beach.

Paris

Paris is a very walkable city, making it perfect for solo travelers. A Paris Visite travel card, which costs money, offers unlimited excursions for a certain number of days, and public transportation choices like the Métro and bus system are also simple to use. Find a location along the Seine to enjoy a baguette and a bottle of wine like a native in Paris. You can also get a Paris Museum Pass and explore the incredible artwork in the Musée du Louvre, the Centre Pompidou, and the Musée d'Orsay (try Friday night when it opens later to avoid crowds).

Remember that on Mondays or Tuesdays, most museums and monuments are often closed. On the Right Bank, the Hotel Indigo Paris - Opera is accessible to several attractions, while the Left Bank is home to many attractive vacation apartments. The city also has a wide selection of inexpensive hostels where you may meet other lone travelers.

San Diego

San Diego, California, appeals to a wide range of single travelers due to its abundance of places to see and things to do. Visitors may surf and sunbathe at Pacific Beach, then go to La Jolla for shopping and a close-up look at seals and sea lions, or to the historic Gaslamp Quarter for nightlife. If you like reading comic books, be sure to schedule your solo vacation for July so you can go to Comic-Con International, the biggest annual gathering in the United States devoted to comics and popular culture.

Meanwhile, outdoor enthusiasts may enjoy some California sunshine by trekking through a neighboring state park or exploring the vast Balboa Park and San Diego Zoo. If you're looking for lodging in San Diego, think about booking a room at the famous Hotel del Coronado or choose the La Valencia Hotel near La Jolla for a more tranquil break.

Rome

Every lone traveler should put Rome on their bucket list. The city is home to notable landmarks including the Colosseum and Vatican City, which serves as the headquarters of the Roman Catholic Church and is the world's smallest sovereign state. It's simple to mingle and go about on your own in Italy since the population tends to speak English and is typically nice and welcoming. Even with a Roma Pass, which provides free public transit and discounted access to over 45 well-liked tourist locations, the bus system may be a handy form of transportation (albeit buses can become busy during the height of summer travel).

Several handy lodging alternatives, like the Aleph Rome Hotel and the Hotel Indigo Rome - St. George on Via Giulia, one of Rome's most picturesque streets, are located in the city's center close to well-known Rome landmarks like Trastevere and the Spanish Steps. It's also simple to visit the city using hop-on/hop-off services like The Roman Guy, who, among other things, provides trips to the Colosseum's underground chambers and the city's ancient catacombs.

Santa Fe, New Mexico

Solo visitors can think about going to Santa Fe if they want a bright sky and a relaxed vacation. The oldest capital of the United States, this Southwestern city has an average of 325 days of sunshine per year, a plethora of attractions, and a vibrant art scene. Visitors may go skiing or hiking, explore the historic Canyon Road, the center of Santa Fe's art scene, or visit more than 20 museums, including the Georgia O'Keeffe Museum. You have a few options for getting to the city: driving there, taking a flight into Santa

Fe Regional Airport, or taking a flight into Albuquerque International Sunport, where Groome Transportation provides shuttles to Santa Fe. Then, visitors may navigate the area on foot, by bicycle, or by using the city's transit system.

Asheville, North Carolina

Asheville, located in the Blue Ridge Mountains of North Carolina, is a welcoming, art-focused mountain town that also happens to be the location of the 8,000-acre Biltmore Estate, once owned by George Vanderbilt. In addition to providing chances for solo hiking, bicycling, kayaking, and fly fishing, the city has more than 100 art galleries. Asheville is a terrific spot to discover exciting and quirky restaurants and savor regional beers since it has the fastest-growing culinary scene and the most breweries per capita of any American city.

Check out the opulent Omni Grove Park Inn or the accommodations of the Biltmore Estate, which include The Inn on Biltmore Estate and the Village Hotel. Asheville Regional Airport is serviced by several domestic airlines, but many East Coast visitors may easily get there by automobile, making it a fantastic choice for solo day trips or weekend vacations.

Tuscany, Italy

Consider taking a stroll along the Via Francigena, a historic pilgrimage path that passes through most of Tuscany, including well-known hill towns like Siena and San Gimignano, for the perfect solitary retreat. In her book "Return to Glow: A Pilgrimage of Transformation in Italy," American author Chandi Wyant, who resides in Italy, recalls her experience trekking the walk alone and how she encountered kind people who assisted her along the way. Since English is a common language and there are several activities available, VBT Bicycling Vacations also suggests Tuscany to visitors who are traveling alone. Additionally, the many Italian trattorias in each town are sure to welcome everyone with open arms and plenty of charcuterie and wine.

Santa Barbara, California

Experience world-class shopping, wine tasting, and beauty in Santa Barbara, a city in California noted for its red-tiled roofed buildings and several paseos (secret pathways) that go deep beneath State Street, the city's main road. While the Old Mission Santa Barbara highlights the city's rich history, the Funk Zone neighborhood has wine tastings, nightlife, and art.

Other enjoyable pursuits include wine tasting in surrounding towns like Los Olivos and Solvang and hiking in the Santa Ynez Mountains. Check out prestigious Santa Barbara hotels like the Four Seasons Resort The Biltmore Santa Barbara and the opulent Kimpton Canary Hotel, or choose a peaceful bed & breakfast near to the city center like the quaint Simpson House Inn.

Iceland

Intrepid Travel, a company that organizes group excursions all around the globe, says Iceland is a fantastic location for solo travel. The majority of the population is recognized for being hospitable and speaking English, and the firm also mentions that Wi-Fi and cellular service are both excellent.

Due to the abundance of its natural attractions, which range from glaciers and volcanoes to waterfalls and hot springs, the nation is sometimes referred to as the Land of Fire and Ice. Consider traveling there in the summer to take advantage of the practically constant daylight and engage in outdoor activities like ice climbing, caving, cycling, and hiking.

The capital and largest city of Iceland, Reykjavik, makes for a convenient home base due to its proximity to the country's international airport and its abundance of stores, cafés, museums, and art galleries. There are many conventional lodging options in metropolitan areas, but camping and Airbnb are the best options in Iceland's tiny villages.

New York City

Due to its enormous cultural diversity, this city is a well-liked choice for lone travelers with a variety of interests. New York City is simple to get to and visit, with three airports, two main Manhattan rail stations, and a subway system that gets you almost wherever you want to go. Avoid Times Square and instead explore less crowded locations like the fashionable Brooklyn, the lovely West Village, and the stylish Meatpacking District. For a breathtaking perspective of the Manhattan skyline, travel over the elevated pedestrian walkway of the Brooklyn Bridge.

After your tour, get a piece of New York-style pizza at a nearby restaurant like Joe's Pizza before retiring for the evening. Hotels in New York include the Hotel Elysée in Midtown, The Williamsburg Hotel in Brooklyn, and Gansevoort Meatpacking NYC.

Toronto

The Canadian metropolis of Toronto located roughly 100 miles north of Buffalo, New York, gives a uniquely European atmosphere close to home. utilize the GO Transit system of trains, buses, and streetcars to get about the city. If you choose to stay in the downtown area, you may utilize the PATH, a network of mostly underground pedestrian walkways, to get around. The CN Tower, one of the highest structures in the world at around 1,815 feet, Yonge-Dundas Square, the CF Toronto Eaton Centre, and the Toronto Zoo are some of the top attractions.

Download Pass TO Savings, a free mobile pass that offers discounts on the city's greatest attractions and activities, or buy the Toronto CityPASS to quickly view several attractions for a discounted price and skip lengthy ticket lines. Visit Centre Island, which is less than 3 miles south of the city center, or High Park, Toronto's biggest public park, if you'd like to spend time outside.

Seville, Spain

Plan a solo vacation to Seville, the capital of Spain's autonomous Andalusia province, for a taste of the nation. Seville is quite easy to get about because of its huge bus system and one metro line. The Catedral de Sevilla, the Torre del Oro and La Giralda towers, and Alameda de Hércules Park are prominent city landmarks that are located in the center of the city. Once the sun has fallen, explore the Triana and Alameda areas' nightlife. Make sure you include time for a football (soccer) game or a flamenco dancing instruction.

Naples, Florida

Naples, located on Florida's Gulf Coast, is known for its abundant sunlight, immaculate beaches, and upscale lifestyle. Visitors may fly into Fort Myers's Southwest Florida International Airport, which is roughly 35 miles north of the city, to reach the city. After arriving in Naples by car, lone travelers may visit the beach or one of the upmarket stores and restaurants that line Third Street South and Fifth Avenue South in the city's renowned historic district. Visitors may treat themselves to a stay at one of the area's opulent hotels, such as the Naples Grande Beach Resort or the Inn on Fifth.

Ljubljana, Slovenia

The Slovenian capital, in contrast to other European towns, provides breathtaking landscapes without throngs of people, making it an excellent holiday spot for individuals traveling alone. Join a two-hour tour of the old city center and Ljubljana Castle, which includes a trip up the funicular to the castle, to gain your bearings.

Additionally, you may visit the Dragon and Triple Bridges on a boat tour of the Ljubljanica River, stroll around Tivoli Park, or explore the 2,000-year-old Roman city's remains. You may visit more than 20 local sites with the practical Ljubljana Card, plus you get unlimited access to public transit and free WiFi. Travel around 35 miles northwest to Bled to visit its breathtaking lake and 11th-century castle if you become tired of Ljubljana's many attractions.

Seattle

Visit the Pacific Northwest to see this dynamic city filled with breathtaking natural scenery. Take the Link light rail from the airport to downtown if you're coming by aircraft. To move about the city, you may also use the buses, streetcars, or monorail (think about getting an ORCA day ticket for unlimited trips on most means of transit).

From the recognizable Space Needle to the busy Pike Place Market, where the first Starbucks shop is situated, there are many sights and activities to enjoy in Seattle. Visit Snoqualmie Falls, stroll around the 9-acre Olympic Sculpture Park, or arrange a whale-watching tour for a taste of nature. A stay at a prestigious Seattle hotel, such as the Hotel 1000 or the beachfront Edgewater Hotel, is a must for any trip there.

Vietnam

InsideAsia Tours advises taking a holiday in Vietnam if you want to travel alone in Asia. Although InsideAsia does advise traveling with or meeting up with an English-speaking guide to help you get your bearings and schedule activities, the tour operator describes Vietnam as a safe location with friendly people and excellent food.

Make sure to sample well-known meals like pho (a rice noodle soup) and bun cha (a dish with noodles and grilled pork). Discover Ho Chi Minh City, the nation's capital, and its museums, temples, pagodas, and parks by foot, by city bus, or by local train for attractions.

Thailand

Bangkok and other popular cities in Thailand, according to many travel blogs, are safe for lone travelers. Top attractions in the Thai capital include the appropriately titled Grand Palace, the gourmet haven of Khao San Road, as well as a vibrant nightlife. Visitors to Thailand may make use of the many transportation options available there, which vary from international alternatives like trains, subways, buses, and taxis to regional options like long-tail boats and three-wheeled motorbikes known as tuk-tuks.

Women who are alone travelers may even download the "Women's Journey Thailand" app from the Tourism Authority of Thailand for extra advice.

Portland, Oregon

Portland is a great destination for lone travelers because of its reputation for having liberal and open-minded citizens. Additionally, it's the best place to go for "weird" (always praise in

Portland) tourists wishing to experience a similar culture. To go from point A to point B, think about bicycling (it's a local favorite), using the MAX Light Rail, or riding the Portland Streetcar. On a beer tour or a low-key night out, don't forget to try some of the city's regional beers. Portland, known as "Beervana" for its outstanding craft beer sector, has more than 70 breweries.

Portland also has fantastic places to go alone including the Portland Japanese Garden and Powell's City of Books, as well as hip areas like the Pearl District, Hawthorne, and Belmont. Visit Voodoo Doughnut to sample doughnuts with toppings like Captain Crunch and bacon. The Royal Sonesta Portland Downtown Hotel and The Porter Portland are two trendy city hotels worth seeing.

New Zealand

New Zealand is a great choice for solo travelers since it is often referred to be one of the safest and nicest nations in the world and hence one of the finest destinations to travel alone. This island country entices outdoor enthusiasts with its stunning landscapes, which have been portrayed in movies like "The Lord of the Rings" and "A Wrinkle in Time." You may take your time discovering its numerous national parks, glowworm caverns, hot springs, and black sand beaches.

To see ancient Arrowtown, taste wine in the vineyards of Gibbston Valley, and shop while admiring Lake Wakatipu's vistas, base yourself in Queenstown, the world's adventure capital. Adventure seekers interested in trying out sports like skydiving, bungee jumping, and whitewater rafting are also drawn to Queenstown. Rent a vehicle or get an InterCity FlexiPass to travel by bus between cities; use a plane or boat to travel between the North and South islands of the nation.

Hostels in New Zealand's main cities and villages that are inexpensive and well-liked by tourists provide several chances to form friendships with other travelers.

Morocco

Consider an Intrepid Travel tour in Morocco if you're organizing your vacation. The "Best of Morocco" itinerary for lone travelers includes trekking in the Atlas Mountains, riding a camel in the Sahara Desert, exploring Marrakech's spice shops, and taking in Casablanca's stunning architecture.

This journey is perfect for anyone who prefers traveling in a group with other solo travelers rather than visiting entirely on their own, even though most of the nation may be friendly to outsiders.

Galápagos Islands

From Guayaquil and Quito in Ecuador, you may take a flight to this group of islands, which is a safe natural paradise famed for its protected species, which includes sea lions, coastal birds, and marine iguanas. The Galápagos Islands need several travel paperwork and an admission charge upon arrival due to current conservation initiatives, thus traveling alone via a tour operator is often the most convenient way to visit.

For several of its National Geographic Endeavour II cruises, Lindblad Expeditions eliminated the single-passenger premium to better accommodate travelers traveling alone. The excursions include several chances to go snorkeling, hiking, kayaking, and taking Zodiac cruises with naturalists.

Charleston, South Carolina

A walkable city, Charleston is home to amiable inhabitants, historic houses, fine dining establishments, and attractive stores. Solo travelers shouldn't pass up the opportunity to cycle or ride in a carriage around the old town. Grand estates like Boone Hall Plantation & Gardens and Middleton Place, a 110-acre historical site that tells the whole history of the home's owners, are worth saving time for visiting tourists. Additional must-dos for travelers include taking a boat to Fort Sumter National Monument and going to the South Carolina Aquarium. Consider the HarbourView Inn, which is conveniently placed, for lodging in Charleston, or treat yourself to a gourmet escape with The Restoration's "A Taste of the South" package.

Sydney

Australia's largest city may take some time to get there, but once there, you'll find that there are plenty of things to do and notable places to see. Water sports enthusiasts may surf at beaches like Bondi, Manly, or Cronulla and explore Sydney Harbour. The Royal Botanic Garden, which provides daily free tours, or the Bondi to Coogee Coastal Walk are two options for those looking to take a solo walk.

The famous Sydney Opera House, the Australian National Maritime Museum, and the Sydney Cricket Ground Museum are a few other must-see attractions in the city. All may be reached by light rail, train, bus, or boat. Visitors may get a free, reloadable Opal card with ride discounts to reduce their tickets.

Athens, Greece

Imagine going on your exploration of Greece while admiring its stunning antiques and ruins. The National Archaeological Museum and the Benaki Museum, as well as the well-known Acropolis, a UNESCO World Heritage Site that houses the Parthenon and the Erechtheion, can be found in Athens. Athens is also home to several prestigious institutions.

You may use a trolley bus, bus, or subway to navigate the city, and a tram is available to take you to and from the nearby beaches. The old city center of Athens, one of Europe's biggest pedestrian zones, is perfect for a leisurely evening stroll, as does the seaside. Stop for a drink at a neighborhood café or pub when you need a break from exploring.

New Orleans

Visit Cajun Country while in the lovely metropolis of New Orleans. There are various ways to see this Southern city, but if you're traveling alone, you may want to avoid the late-night Bourbon Street revelry (even if you're a fun-loving person). Beignets, a strong hurricane cocktail, jambalaya, and gumbo are all good places to start.

Following that, you may engage in entertaining and secure activities like a walk around the famed French Quarter, a visit to a nearby cemetery, and a trip on the St. Charles streetcar, the world's oldest streetcar line still in operation. Think about booking a room in a downtown hotel like the opulent Windsor Court or the Mississippi River-facing Hilton New Orleans Riverside.

Austin, Texas

Whether you want to drive, take the bus, MetroRail, rent a bike, or use a pedicab, getting about Austin is simple. This laid-back Texas city is a great destination for solitary travelers because of its strong music culture and creative vibe. Visit one of the more than 250 live music venues, grab a drink on vibrant Sixth Street, or take a stroll along the Lady Bird Lake hiking and bike route. Drive to the Texas Hill Country, which lies outside of the city and has more than 50 wineries and historic villages, if you have a vehicle.

Sri Lanka

People who like nature are drawn to Sri Lanka, which is situated in the Indian Ocean off the southeast coast of India. Eight UNESCO World Heritage Sites, several beautiful beaches, botanical gardens, waterfalls, national parks, and about 500,000 acres of tea farms can all be found on the island. There are railroads, cabs, and air taxis available in the nation to transport you from point A to point B. The capital of Sri Lanka, Colombo, has double-decker buses for tourist excursions as well. Major airlines including Turkish Airlines, Qatar Airways, and Cathay Pacific fly into the island's two international airports, which are serviced by them. Other options for booking vacations to Sri Lanka include travel operators like G Adventures and Audley Travel.

Singapore

Singapore is a worry-free destination for lone travelers because of its well-lit streets and secure public transit system. Additionally, this contemporary city attracts visitors with a variety of interests because of its abundant shopping, vibrant nightlife, and natural wonders. You may stroll through Little India and Chinatown and other areas on foot, or you can peruse the boutiques and stores at one of the many malls along Orchard Road.

Visit the Singapore Botanic Gardens, Gardens by the Bay, or an outlying island to get your fill of greens. You may get to this city by foot, bicycle, bus, or MRT (Mass Rapid Transit) rail. To avoid penalties, be careful to check local rules before your trip (such as if chewing gum is allowed or not).

San Francisco

Thanks to San Francisco's substantial international airport, cable cars, streetcars, trains, and buses, getting about the city independently is a breeze. Adding a hop-on/hop-off Big Bus sightseeing trip over the Golden Gate Bridge, touring Telegraph Hill's Coit Tower, and strolling through the city's historic Chinatown area to your solo schedule are must-do activities.

After working up an appetite, have a traditional seafood supper at the Fog Harbor Fish House (which has a bay view) before checking into one of San Francisco's premier hotels for the evening, such as the Palace Hotel, Hotel Zoe Fisherman's Wharf, or another.

Ireland

It will be difficult for solo visitors to find a place as welcoming and simple to navigate as the Republic of Ireland. Travel is a breeze thanks to the friendly people and the good public transit system in the nation. Fly into one of Ireland's five international airports, then take the rail for intra city travel, a local bus to see the surrounding area, or a rental vehicle for more independent travel.

Dublin, the capital of Ireland, is home to the Guinness Storehouse, Dublin Castle, and a booming music and nightlife scene. Visit Galway, a UNESCO City of Film with a bohemian feel, to take advantage of stylish shops, mouthwatering cuisine, and convenient access to some of Ireland's must-see scenery. Connemara, the Cliffs of Moher, and the Aran Islands are essential destinations for any tourist. To view the recognizable Blarney Castle, go to County Cork in the south of Ireland.

While kissing the Blarney Stone is a must-do, visitors shouldn't skip the ancient site's grounds, which include the intriguing Poison Garden. Enjoy a luxurious stay in Ireland at Ballyvolane House, Glenlo Abbey Hotel & Estate, or The Shelbourne, or reserve a bed-and-breakfast for a more intimate experience.

Munich, Germany

Munich is often associated with Oktoberfest, the biggest public celebration in the world, so you wouldn't be alone if that were the case. This German city is perhaps best known for its annual Bavarian festival, which features beer, pretzels, and Lederhosen, but it's a wonderful destination all year round for single travelers.

The 27 separate districts of the city are accessible by foot, bus, streetcar (Straßenbahn), underground train (U-Bahn), and aboveground rail (S-Bahn). With a Munich Card, you may take advantage of free local transportation on these services as well as significant savings on more than 100 offers for dining, museums, shopping, and other activities.

Visit the well-known Glockenspiel in the city's center, stroll around Marienplatz and Viktualienmarkt, or climb to the observation deck of the Munich Town Hall Tower for a bird's-eye perspective of the area. In the vast parklands that make up the city, you may also get a breath of fresh air; the English Garden, for instance, is Germany's biggest urban park.

Soccer games, or football as it is called in Germany, are available at the Allianz Arena, and visitors may also take tours of Olympiapark, the location of the 1972 Summer Olympics, and the FC Bayern Museum.

Florianópolis, Brazil

Travelers are not unfamiliar with Brazil. Rio de Janeiro and Sao Paolo are well-known tourist attractions, but solo travelers should exercise caution in Brazil, according to travel blogs. Safety may be an issue in these large cities for solitary travelers. On the other side, tourists often hail Brazil's sun-drenched Florianópolis (also known as Floripa) as one of the most beautiful and secure holiday destinations in the world.

More than 40 beaches in Floripa include walking routes, diving, and paragliding. Visit Joaquina

Beach for surfing and breathtaking dawn views, or spend a peaceful day hiking the trails of Lagoinha do Leste (one of Brazil's finest beaches). Head to Jurerê Beach in the evening for a taste of Floripa's nightlife and delicious seafood; guests claim the oysters here are unrivaled.

One of the most well-liked tourist spots in Brazil is Iguaçu Falls, which is easily accessible from Floripa: It is higher than Niagara Falls and broader than Victoria Falls, and it has 275 spectacular waterfalls. With G Adventures' "Iguassu Falls Independent Adventure," a four-day trip that is specially created for solo travelers, there is no single extra to pay to view this breathtaking natural marvel. Simply jump on a quick flight and take your travels to the next level. You will get the opportunity to see both the Argentine and Brazilian sides of the falls on your outing.

Chapter 4: 20 Solo Travel Mistakes You Must Avoid

I like traveling alone, and it has made for some of my finest experiences. I've been to several wonderful nations in Europe and even ones that are regarded as hazardous in Latin America. Solo travel may be an enriching and transformative experience. When you first go out on your own, you even believe you can do anything.

But I've learned a few things through my trips and my errors along the road. Continue reading to learn about some mistakes I and other lone travelers have made. Maybe this list can help you stay away from them.

- **Making An Incorrect Hotel Reservation**

This is one of the most important aspects of traveling, even if you'll be out exploring more than just relaxing in your accommodation. Saving money might be appealing, but having a hotel that is cozy, secure, has a front desk open around the clock, and is in the correct location can make your stay more enjoyable. But once again, the key objective is to feel secure when traveling alone.

Booking a hotel takes up the most time for me when I'm making vacation plans since I check out all the reviews, compare costs, look at maps, and consider all the options. But as a result of doing that, I've had very few negative encounters. Additionally, numerous excellently rated hotels and hostels with wonderful rates even include breakfast.

- **Listening to People**

You will hear individuals explain to you the many reasons a nation is unsafe while you are traveling there. The saddest aspect is that they have never visited. They just finished watching the news. Keep your fear from keeping you from going. You can lose out on seeing a wonderful nation.

I've been to places like Colombia, Mexico, and Guatemala that have a bad reputation for safety, and I had the best time ever there.

- **Not Seeking Assistance**

The ability to ask for assistance is a skill that may be acquired via solitary travel. I resolve issues on my own at home. However, it's simple for me to feel lost and bewildered when I'm in a new city. Become used to requesting directions from locals.

Don't be hesitant to message regional Instagram travel influencers. Send a message to someone you know who just visited and ask for advice. Make friends with the hotel employees and ask for advice from them.

- **Not Keeping to Budget**

You may make your solo trip as inexpensive or as pricey as you choose. Therefore, if you want to save money, having a strategy is crucial. While planning your vacation, research the best and most affordable restaurants, accommodations, and activities instead of planning every little detail. In this manner, you will be aware of which regions to avoid due to the high pricing when you arrive.

- **Overpacking**

When you travel alone, you are the only one who carries your belongings. I can assure you that it is not enjoyable to carry a big bag through the airport or to carry your luggage up five flights of stairs. It drains you. In addition, there are airline regulations, and if you exceed the weight restriction, you will be charged an additional price. If at all feasible, consider taking just a carry-on backpack.

- **Letting Strangers Know You're Alone**

It's OK to tell a tiny falsehood to protect your safety. Avoid mentioning that you're alone to strangers who don't strike you as friendly. Even if it may seem like a casual exchange, you must always put your safety first.

My pals are waiting for me at the hostel, I've informed the drivers. I'll pretend I'm married or that I don't use social media when I run into a man I don't feel comfortable with. It's not necessary to provide specific details or more information about yourself.

- **Staying Away From Locals**

Conversely, strike up a friendship with a total stranger. Though I usually go cautiously, I like establishing acquaintances in the community. Many people who travel alone make the error of merely making acquaintances with other people on the road.

Making friends with the locals allows you to understand more about their way of life, culture, nation, and more. So failing to become friends with them is a mistake. They may also provide you with information on activities and areas to avoid. Additionally, residents are eager to establish acquaintances abroad. Both learning English and educating you in their language are enjoyable for them.

- **A Surplus Of Expectations**

It's simple to assume that everything will be wonderful when traveling alone, but in reality, some days can be awful or dull and others will be quite thrilling. There will be places that everyone will like, but not you.

Or maybe you despise an area that someone else loves. The best course of action is to just show up at each site and take each day as it comes. If you go in with too high of expectations, you could simply be disappointed when it doesn't live up to your hopes.

- **Don't Remain Alone All The Time**

Some individuals see traveling alone as just that—alone. This concept appeals to introverts like myself in a big way. However, you'll pass on fantastic chances to meet new people. It took me some time before I felt comfortable striking up a conversation with a total stranger.

But as time went on, I discovered that a lot of other solo hikers share my sentiments. You may meet some wonderful individuals by stepping outside of your comfort zone and engaging in a conversation; sometimes, you two wind up making new plans since you bonded so well.

Additionally, it's enjoyable to travel and experience places with others. The benefit of meeting people while traveling is that you are not obligated to remain with them if you don't click with them. You owe them nothing, therefore you are free to go on your exploration.

- **Never Wanting To Be Alone**

There's also a flip side to this. Some tourists make the error of never spending any time alone and only engaging in activities when accompanied by someone they meet.

As a consequence, they overlook taking time to relax, think for themselves, read, or study, among other things. Some people even dislike breathing, eating, and walking by themselves. But let me tell you, traveling alone teaches you a lot about who you are.

You discover your likes and dislikes. You develop the ability to speak just to yourself. The nicest part is that you grow to enjoy yourself while learning how to regulate your emotions.

You're not enjoying solitary travel if you always desire to be with someone. Learn to feel at ease being by yourself whether dining out, traveling by bus, or visiting a museum.

- **Unpreparedness For Emergencies**

On a single vacation, a lot of things may, unfortunately, go wrong. Missed flights, minor crimes, or illness are all possibilities. Make sure there is always one person who knows where you are and get travel insurance. Additionally, have additional cash on hand for emergencies.

- **Keeping Valuables Away Unattended**

Most stories that other solo travelers have mentioned about awful things happening to them included them leaving their stuff unattended. So, keep everything in your line of sight.

Don't leave your phone on the restaurant table, pack a waterproof bag for the beach, and keep your valuables in your carry-on. Don't leave your valuables unlocked at a hostel, don't ask a stranger to guard your belongings, and don't hang your handbag from a chair. Although the list may go on forever, the point has been made. Get travel insurance once again, just in case!

- **Overplanning**

If you are on a brief vacation of one week, it's OK if you want to visit everything. Planning every aspect of your trip is a mistake if you're traveling slowly.

You meet a lot of individuals who quickly become close friends when traveling alone. Allowing yourself to be flexible results in you altering your plans so that you may travel together to new locations.

Additionally, when you move to a new city, residents or other travelers could suggest new destinations that the internet didn't inform you about. You can lose out on some wonderful connections or activities if you have a busy schedule.

- **Failure To Conduct Research**

You might waste time and money if you don't complete your research in advance. For instance, several nations have yearly or religious holidays that raise prices or force companies to shut down. When there are a lot of visitors at particular places during the busy season, it might alter your experience and attitude.

If rain, snow, or natural calamities like storms prevent you from carrying out your objectives, it may also put a damper on your plans. Do some research to learn more about what to anticipate.

- **Absence from Groups and Tours**

I'm all for exploring new locations on my own and avoiding tours whenever possible. I was resolved to do everything "solo" when I initially began traveling by myself to save money. I soon learned, though, that it's often preferable to take a local tour and that it's also the greatest way to meet people.

I like being with new people just as much as I enjoy being alone myself. Additionally, there are occasions when it's the quickest and safest method to go there. For instance, I could have traveled alone to save money on several climbs in Peru. However, it may have included getting lost or hanging around for local transportation.

I came to the decision that I would spend a little bit more money on a tour for my safety and to avoid headaches. Since many of the local communities rely on tourism for their survival, taking a tour is also a fantastic opportunity to support them. Large groups, however, might be a drawback of tours, so conduct your homework on the businesses and choose the best fit for you.

- **Not Trying New Things**
-

Some solitary travelers aren't open to exploring new things, even though most are. Many people allow their fear of heights, water, or other things to prevent them from trying new activities.

As a lone traveler, pushing oneself to experience new, uncomfortable things is the greatest thing you can do for yourself. You could come to adore it. And even if you don't like it, you tried.

Food, solo trekking, diving, surfing, camping, and a long list of other new experiences are just a few. Here are some suggestions for exciting solo travel experiences.

- **Forgetting To Drink Within Your Limits**

One of the greatest blunders made by lone travelers is forgetting alcohol limitations. It's good to have fun, but losing your moral compass can put you in situations you might have avoided.

When you consume more alcohol than you should, you open yourself up to attack and robbery. You could get lost or do something foolish or humiliating that you didn't intend to do. Not to mention how costly alcohol is!

- **Leaving drink unattended**

In light of this, I advise all female solo travelers to never leave their drinks unattended. I know I seem a little paranoid, but don't put your confidence in anybody!

Because you can't predict other people's motivations, make sure that if someone buys you a drink, you see the bartender create it and avoid accepting any open drinks.

I once held my drink in my palm while dancing on the Thai island of Koh Phi Phi. One of the men that joined my companion and me in the dance decided to put what seemed to be a pill into my drink.

My first response when I caught him was to shout and hurl my drink at him. I then continued to watch him. I approached him and exposed him while he was dancing with other females. Trust no one, as I have mentioned.

- **Being Tardy**

Exploring is considerably enjoyable and safer when done during the day. But regrettably, violence increases at night in many places. To return to your accommodation before or just a little after sunset, be sure you leave as early as possible.

Try to avoid taking buses that arrive too late at night or too early in the morning when there is no light, and schedule your flights to land in the day if at all feasible.

• Not Practicing Safety Measures

The best course of action isn't always to wing it if you want to be safe. All of the aforementioned measures are preventative measures. Find out what to avoid doing and where to avoid going in the nation you are visiting.

For instance, criticizing the royal family is forbidden in Thailand. Chewing gum is not permitted in Singapore. Then, discussing communism in Cuba is not a good idea. You could end yourself in trouble if you do these things.

Learn the local traditions and conventions, be familiar with emergency phrases, avoid flashing valuables, avoid going out late alone, never risk your safety to save a little money, and keep the aforementioned tips in mind.

Chapter 5: Destinations That Are Safe And Affordable For Solo Travelers

Solo travel is thrilling and challenging, but life is all about conquering these difficulties! Therefore, below additional locations have been added to this book to provide travelers seeking intriguing low-cost solo travel places with more alternatives when planning their trip.

Puerto Rico

Puerto Rico is a cheap Caribbean vacation spot with alluring beaches and an interesting past. Since the US dollar is the official currency, travelers do not need to be concerned about exchange rates or costs. Additionally, direct flights are offered from New York, making access simple and affordable for budget tourists. There are several reasonably priced hotels, guest houses, hostels, and studio flats here that give the protection that lone travelers need to consider.

A journey to Puerto Rico typically costs $218 per day, which includes $18 for local transportation and an average of $39 for one day's worth of food. A 2- or 3-star hotel room costs between $80 and $120 per night. There are many stunning beaches and buildings to discover, and the nation is generally a safe place for travelers to visit. The music and cuisine scenes are also sure to make everyone happy.

Mid-April through June is the ideal time to travel. Puerto Rico attractions include Castillo San Felipe del Morro, Viejo San Juan, Bioluminescent Bay, El Yunque National Forest, and Culebra Island (Playa Flamenco).

Poland

Looking for the least expensive solo trips to Europe? A fantastic holiday filled with fun, excitement, and relaxation may be had in Poland on a budget. One of the most beautiful locations on earth, it offers visitors a variety of thrilling attractions, from breathtaking landscapes to rich history, lively culture, and architectural wonders. Visitors are mesmerized by Poland's breathtaking splendor and are equally excited by a variety of fun outdoor activities.

In Poland, a day typically costs between $60 and USD 75, depending on the housing, transportation, and touring options selected. Meals cost an average of $16 per day, and local transit is $5.91. Additionally, mid-range lodging in Poland costs about $69. So a cheap vacation to Poland is possible!

March to May and September to November are the best months to travel. Visit Warsaw Old Town, Wawel Castle, Kraków, the Auschwitz-Birkenau Memorial and Museum, Malbork Castle, and the Biaowiea Forest National Park among other destinations in Poland.

Slovenia

Slovenia, which is a hidden treasure on a continent full of well-known tourist destinations, is situated in Central Europe. The vibe of Ljubljana, Slovenia, which is reminiscent of Italian towns from fifty years ago but without the exorbitant pricing, would appeal to travelers searching for a budget solo vacation to Europe. Slovenia has access to the Alps outside of the city that is comparable to Switzerland's but without the resort costs (yes, Slovenia is truly substantially less expensive than Switzerland but is perhaps just as gorgeous).

Cities in Slovenia are fairly walkable, which reduces the cost of transportation. Additionally, top-rated hotels often cost less than $60 per night. Between trips, meals will cost less than $15 a plate, which leaves plenty of money to spend on seeing historic sites like the region's castle from the 11th century.

May through October is the ideal time to visit. Lake Bled, Postojna Cave, Ljubljana Castle, Triglav National Park, and Predjama Castle are among the attractions in Ljubljana.

Argentina

Although many tourists have Paris on their bucket lists, the city's exorbitant cost makes it unaffordable for many, especially those going alone and on a tight budget. Buenos Aires, Argentina—often referred to as "The Paris of

South America"—has significant European influences that permeate everything from its architecture to its cuisine and give the city a distinctly European feel at a far lower cost.

Solo travelers may take advantage of the region's intense passion for wine and contemporary cosmopolitan vibe for about $20/night at a hostel in the area's center. The cost of the fusion cuisine, which also combines French and South American elements, with the high-end wine the region is known for, is around $22. Argentina is one of the greatest and safest inexpensive single excursions to do, with attractive European characteristics for a fraction of the expense.

Dec. through Feb. is the ideal time to travel. Visit the La Boca area and Caminito, the Recoleta Cemetery, the Plaza de Mayo and Casa Rosada, the Teatro Colón, the Palermo neighborhood, and the Bosques de Palermo while in Buenos Aires.

Morocco

Morocco is a nation in Africa with a unique mix of traditional and contemporary characteristics. Marrakech, which has a lot of sights and things to do, is where many people start. In addition to contemporary museums and art galleries, this beautiful city is home to mosques, palaces, and gardens.

Due to its secure and reasonably priced rail service, Marrakech is a fantastic base for touring Morocco on your own without having to spend a fortune on rental cars. Hotels in prime areas cost around $68 per night, and for those who do need a cab, the cost is less than $4 for a five-mile ride.

March to May and September to October are the best months to visit. Visit the Jardin Majorelle, the Medina of Marrakech, the Bahia Palace, the Koutoubia Mosque, and Djemaa el-Fna (Main Square) while in Marrakech.

Albania

Albania is a must-visit if you want to get a close-up look at distinctive European architecture, lovely national parks, and distinctive cultural institutions and galleries without paying conventional European costs. The castles built during the Ottoman Empire and the distinctive fusion of Italian, Greek, and Turkish culture will provide solo travelers with plenty of company while they are in Europe.

Hostels may be found for as little as $12 per night in the downtown area, while boutique hotels cost around $43 per night (with breakfast). Visitors may start their days with a coffee for only $1.50 or go downtown for a more upscale brunch for less than $9 per dish.

Optimal Period: June to August. Visit Berat Castle, Butrint National Park, Gjirokastr Castle, Lake Ohrid, and Blue Eye Natural Spring among the tourist attractions in Albania.

Cambodia

Southeast Asia's Cambodia is a tiny yet formidable country. Cambodia somehow goes above and beyond for a place that is already inexpensive and secure. Expect to spend between $3 and $4 for a dinner at a budget restaurant, while street food is often less than $2. Hostels cost as little as $3 a night, while inexpensive hotels that seem luxurious are often less than $50 per night.

If you've grown tired of hostels, consider The Grand Cyclo Boutique & Spa. Even while Cambodia is generally secure, little crimes like stealing and pickpocketing are rather common, so travelers should always be on the alert, just as they would anyplace else.

The best time to travel is from November to April. Angkor Wat, the Royal Palace, Phnom Penh, the Bayon Temple, the Tuol Sleng Genocide Museum, and the Killing Fields at Choeung Ek are among the attractions of Cambodia.

Malaysia

Malaysia is one of the most stunning and affordable locations to travel alone on a budget, offering opulent appeal, some of the greatest food in the area, as well as both large cityscapes and tropical beach escapes. Malaysia is the ideal low-cost vacation spot for lone travelers who want to have a good time on a tight budget. For as little as $53 a night, stay in a Kuala Lumpur hotel with a rooftop infinity pool overlooking the Petronas Towers. If you're interested in visiting a beach location, Langkawi, which is famed for its crystal-clear seas and perfect diving, is located just off the coast of Malaysia.

Traveling to Malaysia for the cuisine alone is a good enough excuse; with street foods like curry mee, nasi lemak, and mee goreng mamak, the country's delights will have visitors coming back for more. The fact that typical street food costs $2 to $3 in this area will help keep customers coming back for more.

Although Malaysia is generally a safe place to visit, ladies should especially be aware that they may likely draw attention to themselves. Although women are not required to cover themselves fully, wearing modest clothing will probably deter any unwanted attention.

The best time to travel is from February through September. The Petronas Twin Towers, Mount Kinabalu, Langkawi Island, Georgetown, Penang, and Taman Negara

National Park are among the attractions of Malaysia.
Peru

Want to see a global wonder while traveling in safety and on a tight budget? Then it's time to get a plane ticket to Peru! A terrific place to visit for history, scenery, gastronomy, and culture in Peru. Prepare to see some llamas and alpacas ambling about the area as they own it. Discover the past of the Achuar, Aguaruna, Asháninka, Shipibo, Huambisa, Quechua, and Aymara indigenous peoples of Peru. Enjoy Machu Picchu's views, one of the world's newest marvels, which may be accessed on a day trip or by hiking the notorious and difficult Inca Trail.

Visit Vinicunca and take a hike up the spectacular Rainbow Mountain. Have no fear, solo travelers: Peru is one of the most popular travel destinations for backpackers. While common sense should always be used, it is generally a great location for a solo getaway in terms of cost, safety, and memorable experiences. Avoid situations where tourists may be more vulnerable, such as getting drunk.

The best time to go is from May through October. Attractions: Lake Titicaca, Colca Canyon, Nazca Lines, Sacred Valley of the Incas, Machu Picchu

Colombia

Due to a small number of negative actors, certain regions are grossly misrepresented, and for the longest time, Colombia came in close second. The days when Colombia should be avoided are long gone. With a record-breaking 4.5 million tourists in 2019, Colombia saw its greatest rates of tourism to date before the Covid-19 epidemic hit the whole planet.

This is primarily due to Colombia's vibrant environment, which includes the undulating hills of Medelln and the vibrant streets of Cartagena, its mouthwatering cuisine (the arepas served from Columbian food carts are genuinely unique), and its stringent security measures. Even female visitors traveling alone have admitted that Colombia is one of their top picks for safety.

Dec. through March is the ideal time to travel. Colombia's tourist attractions include the Old Town of Cartagena, Tayrona National Park, the Metrocable in Medellin, the Coffee Cultural Landscape, and the Gold Museum in Bogota.

Guatemala

Due to the mistaken perception that it is
dangerous and uninteresting to go there, Central

America is an underappreciated location. Affordability is undoubtedly one of the reasons to go to Central America. The underestimated country of Guatemala manages to squeak up to becoming one of the cheapest countries in a part of the world that is already rather inexpensive. Traveling through Guatemala is fantastic since it's a small country, so the more time you have, the better. For those with a limited amount of time, Guatemala may easily be visited in only a few days.

Take a walk around the Spanish colonial districts of Antigua's old town. Lake Atitlán, which consistently ranks near the top of lists of the world's most beautiful lakes, has fantastic views of Volcan Atitlán. Have the time of one's life in stunning Guatemala and silence the doubters about "dangerous" Central America.

November through April are the best months to travel. Tikal National Park, Lake Atitlán, Antigua Guatemala, Semuc Champey, and Pacaya Volcano are among the attractions of Guatemala.

Mexico

Speaking of nations that are inaccurately depicted in Western media, Mexico is a stunningly accessible and generally safe country to consider for a solo vacation. Avoid the expensive Tulum tourist area and go to Sayulita, a beach hamlet in western Mexico. Are you looking for a place where you can eat some of the greatest street cuisine in the world? The best option is Mexico City.

Mexico is a well-known destination, so even lone tourists are likely to run with other travelers along the road. A cheap all-inclusive resort is a terrific option for lone travelers if they are too exhausted to go to Mexico on their own. Mexico demonstrates that being alone when traveling is never truly a bad thing.

December through April is the ideal time to travel. Chichen Itza, Tulum, Palenque, Teotihuacan, and Xcaret Park are among the Mexican tourist attractions.

Portugal

Portugal is a relatively tiny coastal country that offers all of Western Europe's attractiveness without costing an arm and a leg to those who can't afford the exorbitant expenses of Paris or Rome. Portugal is not as cheap as the aforementioned Malaysia or Guatemala, but compared to Western European norms, it is still quite economical.

Explore the winding alleys of Lisbon, taste wine from the adjacent Douro Valley in Porto, then go to Lagos for a reasonably priced lovely beach town. The greatest thing is that Portugal routinely ranks among the safest nations for both travel and residence. Even if it doesn't imply one should let down their guard entirely, one may feel secure knowing they are in one of the safest areas on Earth.

Best Season: March through October. Lisbon, Porto, Sintra, the Algarve, and the Douro Valley are among the destinations in Portugal.

Bulgaria

Despite growing in popularity in recent years, Eastern Europe has plenty of undiscovered attractions and places just waiting to be discovered. Consider visiting the off-the-beaten-track nation of Bulgaria, which has a ton to offer and is simple to reach from popular neighboring countries like Hungary, Turkey, and Greece. With Flixbus, it's easy to hop between nations in Eastern Europe, and buses to Sofia, Bulgaria, can be had for as little as $7 from adjacent towns.

One of the most economical single excursions in Europe for foodies is the capital city of Sofia, where sit-down meals cost, on average, $5 to $7 for a full plate of robust cuisine. Utilize a free walking tour in the city's center to discover Bulgaria's socialist heritage. To get the most out of your money, stay at a hostel where rooms start at about $12 per night. Though Bulgaria has a low crime rate, it is still important to be attentive and aware of one's surroundings.

April to May and September to October are the best months to visit. Bulgaria's tourist attractions include the Rila Monastery, the Alexander Nevsky Cathedral in Sofia, the Old Town of Plovdiv, the Bansko Ski Resort, and the Tsarevets Fortress in Veliko Tarnovo.

Philippines

The Philippines is one of the better alternatives available for a tropical vacation that won't break the wallet. The Philippines may be physically far away, but it is well worth the trip because of its stunning blue oceans, crazy backpacking atmosphere, palm tree-lined highways, and delicious foods like halo-halo, kare kare, and sisig.

When you get there, you can anticipate paying costs that are so cheap you'll wonder why anybody would spend thousands of dollars on overwater bungalows in The Maldives when the Philippines provides the same stunning scenery for a lot less money. The Philippines is one of the simplest countries on earth to meet friends in for single travelers since it is full of sociable, pleasant people. It also helps that the Philippines is among the world's top Instagrammable locations.

Dec. through Feb. is the ideal time to travel. Visit Boracay Island, Chocolate Hills, Mayon Volcano, Palawan Underground River, and Tubbataha Reefs Natural Park among the Philippines' top tourist destinations.

Taiwan

Taiwan tops the list for individuals seeking a location that is both contemporary and historical, morally liberal but with traditional values, vibrant and yet naturally beautiful, and secure but accessible. The nation's capital, Taipei, is a terrific place to buy, dine, and socialize with the locals. It is widely renowned for its late-night Taiwanese markets.

At a price that won't force guests to hunt for a second job when they return from their vacation, Taipei offers a vibe that is somewhat reminiscent of Tokyo or Seoul. Taiwan is particularly fantastic for traveling alone since it is well-known for being safe, and even better, a recent movement has made it safe for LGBTQIA+ visitors, making it one of the most LGBTQIA+-friendly nations in Asia. A location that is safe for all sorts of tourists deserves commendation and, more importantly, should be visited.

Optimal Season: June through August. Visit Taroko National Park, Taipei 101, Sun Moon Lake, Alishan National Scenic Area, and Kenting National Park among the tourist attractions in Taiwan.